W9-DIU-206

# Surviving an Earthquake

by Heather Adamson

amicus readers

2

# amicus readers

## Say hello to amicus readers.

You'll find our helpful dog, Amicus, chasing a ball—to let you know the reading level of a book.

# A

**Learn to Read**

Frequent repetition of sentence structures, high frequency words, and familiar topics provide ample support for brand new readers. Approximately 100 words.

# 1

**Read Independently**

Repetition is mixed with varied sentence structures and 6 to 8 content words per book are introduced with photo label and picture glossary supports. Approximately 150 words.

# 2

**Read to Know More**

These books feature a higher text load with additional nonfiction features such as more photos, time lines, and text divided into sections. Approximately 250 words.

Amicus Readers are published by Amicus
P.O. Box 1329, Mankato, Minnesota 56002
www.amicuspublishing.us

U.S. publication copyright © 2012 Amicus.
International copyright reserved in all countries.
No part of this book may be reproduced in any
form without written permission from the publisher.

Printed in the United States of America at at Corporate
Graphics, in North Mankato, Minnesota.

Series Editor          Rebecca Glaser
Series Designer        Bobbi J. Wyss
Photo Researcher       Heather Dreisbach

Library of Congress Cataloging-in-Publication Data
Adamson, Heather, 1974-
  Surviving an earthquake / by Heather Adamson.
    p. cm. – (Amicus Readers. Be prepared)
  Includes index.
  Summary: "Discusses the dangers of earthquakes, how
to prepare for them, and how to stay safe during and
after an earthquake"– Provided by publisher.
  ISBN 978-1-60753-148-7 (library binding)
  1. Earthquakes-Juvenile literature. 2. Earthquakes-
Safety measures-Juvenile literature. I. Title.
  QE521.3.A335 2011
  613.6'9-dc22
                                        2010049880

Photo Credits
Martin Hunter/Getty Images, Cover; Code Red/Getty Images, 1; Luciano Corbella/Getty Images, 4, 21m;
Kevin Schafer/Getty Images, 5; JONATHAN NOUROK/AFP/Getty Images, 7, 20b; TED ALJIBE/AFP/Getty
Images, 8; Sandra SEBASTIAN/AFP/Getty Images, 9, 21b; Caro / Alamy, 11; Maroš Markovi 1 Dreamstime.
com, 13; David McNew/Getty Images, 15, 21t; Marty Melville/AFP/Getty Images, 17; Furchin/iStockphoto,
18, 20t; IAIN MCGREGOR/AFP/Getty Images, 19; manley099/iStockphoto, 22

1035    3-2011
10 9 8 7 6 5 4 3 2 1

# Table of Contents

Earthquakes                          4

Preparing for an Earthquake          10

During an Earthquake                 14

After an Earthquake                  16

Photo Glossary                       20

Activity: Earthquake Plans           22

Ideas for Parents and Teachers       23

Index and Web Sites                  24

# Earthquakes

Earthquakes make the ground shake and ripple. Large **plates** of rock shift and bump deep underground. This movement of the earth can be dangerous.

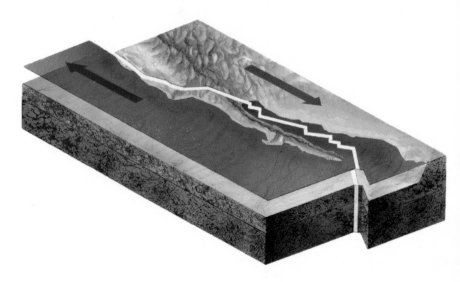

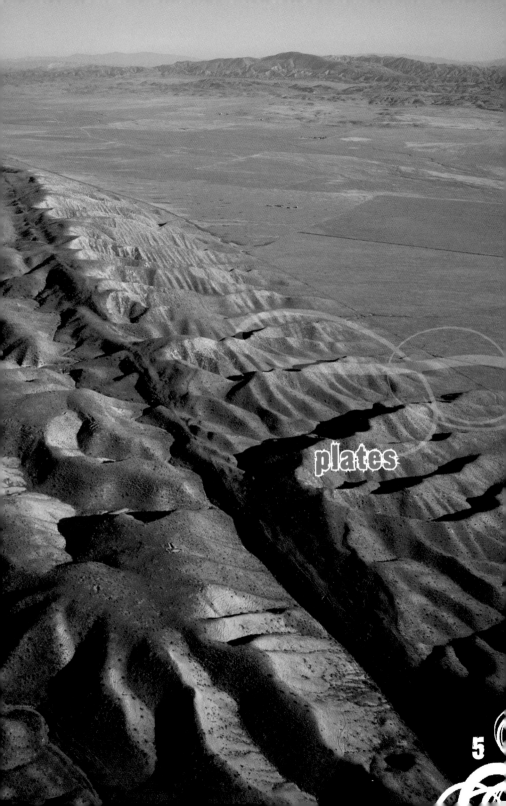

plates

When the ground shakes, things may fall or break. Buildings, roads, and homes can be wrecked in just a few quaking minutes. People can be hurt from the **debris**.

debris

**Scientists** study how the earth moves, but they don't know when earthquakes will happen. There are no warnings for earthquakes. But places near shifting plates are more likely to have earthquakes.

scientist

9

# Preparing for an Earthquake

Earthquake plans help people be prepared for an earthquake. Part of the plan is getting buildings ready.

For example, bolt shelves to the wall. Store heavy items on low shelves. Then they won't fall on you.

Plan where to go. Find spots in each room where you are protected from falling debris. Under a table is a good choice. Find places away from windows and things that could fall easily.

Practice earthquake drills so you know what to do during an earthquake.

not safe

safe

13

# During an Earthquake

During an earthquake, you should drop, cover, and hold. Stop what you are doing and drop to the floor. Then get under a covering such as a table, desk, or chair. Hold on to your covering until the shaking stops.

# After an Earthquake

When the shaking stops, you must be careful. Cracked walls or buildings may still fall.

If you are stuck, stay calm. Tap a pipe or blow a whistle to call for help. Do not scream unless you have no other way to make noise.

**Aftershocks** often happen after big earthquakes. These smaller quakes can happen for a few weeks. You may need to go somewhere safe until the shaking is done. Earthquakes are scary, but knowing what to do will help you stay safe.

aftershock

# Photo Glossary

## aftershocks
smaller earthquakes that happen after the main earthquake

## debris
broken pieces of glass or damaged buildings

## drill
to practice what you
would do in an emergency

## plates
layers of rock underground;
they are like earth's shell.

## scientists
someone who studies
science; earthquake scientists
are called seismologists.

# Activity: Earthquake Plans

What are good places in this room to take cover during an earthquake?

A and D are good choices. The dining table and doorway will protect you from falling items and give you something to hold on to. B and C are not good choices because they are near windows and glass that could fall on you.

# Ideas for Parents and Teachers

*Be Prepared*, an Amicus Readers Level 2 series, provides simple explanations of what storms are and offers reassuring steps that kids and families can take to be prepared for disasters. As you read this book with your children or students, use the ideas below to help them get even more out of their reading experience.

## Before Reading

* Read the title and ask the students if they've ever experienced an earthquake or know someone who has.

* Ask the students why they need to be prepared for earthquakes.

* Use the photo glossary words to help them predict what they will learn from the book.

## Read the Book

* Ask the students to read the book independently.

* Provide support where necessary. Point out that the photo labels can help them learn new words.

## After Reading

* Ask the students to retell what they learned about earthquakes and how to prepare for them. Compare their answers to what they said before reading the book.

* Have students do the activity on page 22 and talk about earthquake plans in your own home or school.

# Index

aftershocks 18
being stuck 16
buildings 6, 16
debris 6, 12
drills 12
drop, cover, and hold 14
earthquake plans 10

homes 6
plates 4, 8
roads 6
safe places 12
scientists 8
warnings 8

# Web Sites

**Beat the Quake--The Great Southern California ShakeOut**
http://www.dropcoverholdon.org/beatthequake/

**DragonflyTV Episodes. Earth and Space. Earthquakes**
http://pbskids.org/dragonflytv/show/earthquakes.html

**Earthquakes for Kids (USGS)**
http://earthquake.usgs.gov/learn/kids/

**FEMA for Kids—Disaster Connection**
http://www.fema.gov/kids/quake.htm